Jean Tennant's

"WRITERS' SEMINAR & WORKSHOP"

Course Materials

Published by: Shapato Publishing
            PO Box 476
            Everly, IA 51338

ISBN: 978-0-9821058-3-2
Copyright © 2009 Shapato Publishing

First Printing June 2009

SYLLABUS

THE AUTHOR'S LIFESTYLE

QUALITIES NEEDED TO BECOME A SUCCESSFUL WRITER

WRITERS' EQUIPMENT AND SUPPLIES

SHARPENING YOUR WRITING SKILLS
   Word Selection / Sentence Structure / Paragraph Structure /
   Self-Editing

YOUR GREAT MANUSCRIPT IDEA
   Sources of Ideas / Developing an Idea / Testing Your Idea

WRITING POSSIBILITIES
   Markets / Genres

MANUSCRIPT DEVELOPMENT
   Target Market / Outline / Title / Pen Names

MANUSCRIPT MECHANICS
   Formatting

SUBMITTING YOUR WORK
   Finding the Right Publisher / Writing a Query Letter or Cover
   Letter / Multiple Submissions? / Realistic Expectations

LITERARY AGENTS

THE AUTHOR'S CONTRACT

PROTECTING YOUR WORK
   How to Copyright Your Manuscript

QUESTION AND ANSWER SESSION

PARTICIPANTS' WORK-SHARING SESSION

4

THE AUTHOR'S LIFESTYLE

1. Solitude

   Are you prepared to spend long periods of time sequestered?

2. Questions

   People will want to know what you're working on. It's up to you to decide if you want to answer those questions.

3. Criticism

   Is your family supportive?

4. Time factor

   It can take months or even years to write a full-length book. Are you prepared for that?

5. Facing Rejection

   It's inevitable, and painful. Can you take it?

> "Writing is easy. All you do is sit staring at a blank sheet of paper until drops of blood form on your forehead."
> Gene Fowler

QUALITIES NEEDED TO BE A SUCCESSFUL WRITER

IDEAL PERSONAL QUALITIES

1. The Dream / The Desire / Determination
2. Curiosity
3. Organizational Ability
4. Self-Discipline
5. Dedication to Factual Accuracy
6. Persistence / Perseverance
7. Ability to Work Alone
8. Inspiration
9. Enthusiasm
10. Ability to Work Under Pressure
11. Willingness to Accept Constructive Criticism
12. Cooperative Nature
13. Patience
14. Perspective
15. Energy
16. Survival Money

> "Young minds are always hungry for a good story, and with children I feel my words are truly understood and appreciated." Judy Blume

TECHNICAL SKILLS

1. Command of English language: spelling, punctuation, etc.
2. Ability to clearly communicate your ideas in writing
3. Knowledge of Manuscript Format
4. Knowledge of the Markets
5. Keyboarding Ability

THE WRITER'S EQUIPMENT AND SUPPLIES

SUGGESTED EQUIPMENT AND SUPPLIES

1. An Idea

2. Paper

3. Envelopes

4. Word Processing Program or Typewriter

5. Ideas File

6. Information File

7. Quiet Place to Write

8. Reference Books

   a. Dictionary / Thesaurus

   b. Style Manual

   c. Specific Books in Your Subject Area

   d. Books that describe how to write your particular type of material

   e. Market Guides

9. Printer or Access to Copy Machine

10. Program or Book to Record Expenses

11. Personalized Business Stationery (optional)

12. Business Cards (optional)

> "A professional writer is an amateur who didn't quit."
>   Richard Bach

SHARPENING YOUR WRITING SKILLS

WORD SELECTION

Use words that convey what you want them to say.

Use words that have precise meaning.

Use short, simple, easy-to-understand words instead of long, complicated, or technical words.

Don't write down to your readers.

Select words that are within your readers' comprehension level.

Visualize a scene or event, then select words to accurately describe it. Paint word-pictures... but don't forget the other senses.

Avoid unnecessary words.

Attributive clauses. When writing dialogue, balance descriptive words and phrases with "said."

"I got a promotion," she _____.

"I don't think that's fair," he _____.

"I'm going to become a doctor," he _____.

"I've gained twenty-five pounds in the last two months," she _____.

"Ouch," he _____.

"Where are you going?" she _____.

"I suppose you're right," he _____.

> "When I have a little money, I buy books.
> If any is left, I buy food and clothes."
>   Erasmus

SENTENCE STRUCTURE

If you don't know rules of grammar, sentence structure and punctuation, look for examples.

Use simple, rather than complicated, sentence structure.

Use sentence structure you can handle.

Vary sentence length.

Write as you would talk, but without the excess words.

Use active, rather than passive, sentences.
      Passive: The 50-yard touchdown pass was thrown by Chuck.
      Active: Chuck threw the 50-yard touchdown pass.

Defining Passive Voice

Passive voice occurs when the subject and object of an action are inverted, so the subject is the recipient of the act instead of its performer. For example:

Passive: The man was bitten by the dog.
Active: The dog bit the man.

Passive: I was told by the interviewer to come at noon.
Active: The interviewer told me to come at noon.

Note that the word "by" is present in these two examples. A sentence can be passive without the word "by," but it is always at least implied. For example: "I was given bad directions [by my friend]."

When Passive Voice is Acceptable

There are generally two cases when passive voice is acceptable: 1) when there is no defined or tangible subject; 2) when the emphasis really should be on the object of the action. In these cases, the alternative is often awkward and sounds less natural.

Case 1: He is called 'the great one.'"
Awkward alternative: "The general public calls him 'the great one.'"

Case 2: "For the fifth time this year, Jefferson was hit by a pitch."
Awkward alternative: "For the fifth time this year, a pitch hit Jefferson."

Avoid clichés and jargon.

Don't overwork the same words (redundancies).

Write for clarity, meaning, and understanding instead of eloquent, but hollow, beauty.

Respect your own "voice."

Choose Strong Action Verbs

Active language comes not just from avoiding passive voice but further requires the use of *strong action verbs*. In addition to avoiding *to be* verbs, you should try to replace helping verbs such as *have, had, has, do, does, did* and other vague verbs like *got* and *get*.

> **Before:** "I **had** opportunities to develop my skills."
> **After:** "I **sought** opportunities to develop my skills."

> **Before:** "I **got** the promotion through hard work."
> **After:** "I **earned** the promotion through hard work."

> **Before:** "She **did well** in this competitive environment."
> **After:** "She **thrived** in this competitive environment."

> **Before:** "My mother **didn't want** to show up without a gift."
> **After:** "My mother **hesitated** to show up without a gift."

> **Before:** "The salesman **told** the audience about his products."
> **After:** "The salesman **promoted** his products to the audience."

The last two examples demonstrate the lack of clear distinction between strong and weak verbs. *Promoted* is simply a stronger word than *told*, and brings the writing to life.

PARAGRAPH STRUCTURE

Present one main topic per paragraph.

Use short paragraphs.

Each sentence in a paragraph should flow smoothly into the next.

Each paragraph should flow smoothly into the next.

SELF-EDITING YOUR WORK

After you finish your manuscript, set it aside for a time. Later, look at it again.

Read your work aloud.

Scrutinize each word, sentence and paragraph.

Read for content and meaning.

Check spelling, punctuation and mechanics.

Check for redundancies.

> "An author in his book must be like God in the universe, present everywhere and visible nowhere."
> Gustave Flaubert

Ask yourself these questions:

Is the sequence of the events and topics logical?
Is the theme believable?
Will a reader get a crystal-clear meaning of my idea?
Is the format consistent?
Is the tone consistent?

Don't stop revising until your work is as good as you can make it.

Expect to revise and rewrite your work 3, 4, 5 times or *more*.

Don't over-edit; seeking perfection can suck the life out of your words.

HONE YOUR WRITING SKILLS

Take college courses.

Attend seminars and workshops.

Read books and magazine articles about writing.

Read and study the type of work you intend to write.

Take online courses in writing, such as those offered by:

> Writer's Digest
> www.writersonlineworkshops.com

Join online writers' groups, such as:

> Coffeehouse for Writers
> www.coffeehouseforwriters.com
>
> Critique Circle
> www.critiquecircle.com
>
> The National Writer's Association
> www.NationalWriters.com

Start your own writers' group.

If you want to be a writer, write!

> Personal letters to friends and relatives
> Keep a journal
> Volunteer to help prepare a newsletter, brochure, or other publication for
>   charitable organizations or a church
> Write stories for children
> Write your family history
> Write letters to the editor

> "I'm not a very good writer, but I'm an excellent rewriter."
> James Michener

YOUR GREAT MANUSCRIPT IDEA

SOURCES OF IDEAS

1. Be curious. Write down every idea that comes to mind.

2. Keep an 'Ideas File.'

3. Analyze your interests and skills.

4. Review your life experiences.

5. Observe everyday life. Be aware of what is happening around you.

6. Observe your family, friends and other people. Watch *and* listen.

7. Observe your community. For what is it famous? What are some interesting facts or stories about its past? What new things are happening? Are any businesses or non-profit organizations doing anything interesting or unusual?

8. Go places. Do things. Broaden your experiences and perspectives. Take a trip. Visit a new locale.

9. Scrutinize newspapers. They'll provide many ideas. Also, they will reveal people's current interests and will show trends.

10. Read. Read books, magazines, newspapers.

11. Study the bestseller lists. They reveal what people are currently buying.

12. With a watchful eye, view television newscasts, documentaries and other programs.

13. With a discriminating ear, listen to the radio.

14. Browse through libraries and bookstores.

15. Scan the *Reader's Guide to Periodical Literature* and the *Subject Guide to Books in Print*, both found in many libraries.

16. Read materials that you wouldn't ordinarily read.

17. Scan the classified ads in newspapers, magazines, tabloids and other publications.

18. Consider these popular nonfiction categories:

    a.   How to make money

    b.   How to make more efficient use of money

    c.   How to eliminate waste

    d.   How to make more efficient use of time

    e.   How to maintain or improve health and appearance

    f.   How to improve happiness

    g.   How to improve personal relationships

    h.   How to make living easier and more enjoyable

    i.   A simplified approach to a difficult task or procedure

    j.   "Secrets" or shortcuts

DEVELOPING AN IDEA

1. Don't lock yourself into preconceived ideas or notions.

2. Be patient. Ideas often develop slowly.

3. If it is a new idea, select the most appropriate approach to telling your story.

4.   If this topic has been written about often, view the basic idea from various viewpoints and angles. Develop a new approach or slant.

5.   View the idea from a reader's perspective. Why would they want to know about this subject? Of what value will it be to them? What type of people would find this interesting?

6.   View the idea from an editor's perspective. Why should they spend time and money publishing it?

7.   Ask yourself these questions: Am I qualified to write about this topic? Do I have the background, experience, education, expertise and credentials to be considered an authority on this topic?

8.   File your idea away and try to forget about it. If it won't go away, it may be worth developing into a manuscript.

TESTING YOUR IDEA

1.   Do an Amazon.com or BarnesandNoble.com search by subject. If there are already many books out on the subject, try to:

   a.   Develop a new slant

   b.   Consider a different forum

2.   If you are in doubt about your idea's salability, send query letters to editors of carefully selected publications to test the waters.

> "Writing is the only thing that, when I do it, I don't feel I should be doing something else."
> Gloria Steinem

WRITING POSSIBILITIES

WRITING MEDIUMS

The following are the most popular writing mediums, and thus are among those with the greatest potential for writing success.

MAGAZINES – ARTICLES

A magazine article is usually 300 to 3,000 words in length, on one of (but not confined to) the following subjects: How-to, technical, historical, interviews, new products and techniques, problem solving, religious experiences, travel, personal experiences.

Advantages

1. There are hundreds of general-interest and special-interest magazines, tabloids and trade journals that could conceivably publish your work.
2. There are thousands of articles purchased from freelance writers each year.
3. Often, dozens of articles are published on the same topic.
4. A relatively small time investment is required per article.
5. There is usually only a small investment in research costs, materials and postage.
6. It's an excellent way to get started as a writer. You can tackle a project with a reasonable prospect of finding success.
7. It's an excellent way to develop publishing credits.
8. It's possible to take a relatively limited idea or specialized topic and develop it into a magazine article.
9. This is often the recommended way to begin as a writer.
10. Potential exists to sell the same article, or similar articles, to several publishers.
11. Potential exists to write many articles on the same subject.
12. Potential exists to write about many different subjects.
13. It's an excellent way to develop writing skills before tackling a bigger project.
14. Potential exists to develop a good magazine article, or series of articles, into a book.

Disadvantages

1. Editors receive many thousands of proposals and it can be difficult to get noticed.
2. Some publishers will not review unsolicited manuscripts.
3. There is a time lag of perhaps four to six months between submission and editor's response.
4. It'll take having many articles published to earn a substantial income.

Income Potential

Major publications pay from $50 to $2,500 for articles of 300 to 3,000 words. The average is about $300 to $500. *Reader's Digest* pays about $5,000 per article. Smaller publications pay smaller amounts and some trade journals do not pay at all.

MAGAZINES – SHORT STORIES

A short story is fiction of approximately 2,500 to 5,000 words. A short-short story is from 500 to 2,000 words.

Advantages

1. Often no technical background, training or expertise is needed.
2. There is unlimited potential for plots and stories.
3. A relatively small time investment is required per story.
4. There's usually a small investment in research costs, materials and postage.
5. It's an excellent way for a beginning writer to sharpen their skills of character development and plot development before trying to write a full-length novel.

Disadvantages

1. The market is more limited than it is for non-fiction articles. Only a few major magazines buy short stories these days. Primarily, the market is with smaller, specialized publications, such as religious and juvenile.
2. Since there is usually no technical background or expertise required, many people select this writing area. Competition can be tough.
3. Some publishers will not review unsolicited manuscripts.

4. There is a time lag of perhaps four to six months between submissions and editor's response.
5. Many book publishers are not interested in publishing collections of short stories, which limits the use of your unpublished (or published) short stories.
6. Many short stories must be published to earn a substantial income.

Income Potential

Major publications pay in the $300 to $1,500 range. Smaller publishers pay much less.

BOOKS – NON-FICTION

These books cover almost every imaginable topic from apples to zoology. Popular topics include business, fitness, gardening, childcare, personal relationships and health. Book length can range from fewer than 100 pages to several hundred pages. Non-fiction works are sold through bookstores (both online and brick-and-mortar), book clubs and direct mail. Libraries are another good market.

Advantages

1. There are hundreds of book publishers. Though many of them prefer certain topics, there are usually several dozen potential publishers for any given topic.
2. It's a great challenge, and a true test of a writer's organizational abilities, endurance and perseverance.
3. A tremendous feeling of accomplishment and self-satisfaction results.
4. There's a high prestige factor.
5. It's possible to easily develop one or more magazine articles based on a book's contents.
6. It's possible to expand to other lucrative and fulfilling ventures.

Disadvantages

1. Books have been written on almost every imaginable topic. A beginning writer needs an outstanding idea and/or unusual approach.
2. Publishers receive thousands of proposals every year. They can be very selective.
3. A writer must ordinarily have the technical training, experience, background and credentials to write an authoritative non-fiction work.

4. A high level of organizational ability is required.
5. A great deal of time is required.
6. A substantial monetary investment may be required for research and materials.
7. If the book does not sell well, the writer's per-hour income will be low.
8. Even if the book does sell well, a time lag of one to two years may exist after the manuscript is completed before royalty income is received.

Income Potential

Income potential can be good. Often, an advance is paid upon signing the contract. This might range from $1,500 to $10,000 for a previously unpublished author. Royalty rates vary, but 10 to 15% of the cover price is a normal range for hardcover books and 6 – 10% is a normal range for paperbacks.

Small publishing companies might pay no advance, but offer higher royalties.

BOOKS – TEXTBOOKS

Textbooks are used for instruction in elementary schools, high schools, vocational-technical schools, junior colleges, universities and specialized institutes. Materials include hardcover books, text-workbooks, workbooks and various types of packets.

Advantages

1. If you have an area of expertise, there are many types of textbooks and educational materials that can be developed in your area.

2. Strong editorial support and assistance is usually provided by the publisher.

3. It's possible to become a new author on a revision, rather than developing your own original manuscript.

4. Major publishers have highly developed, active marketing programs.

5. A successful textbook will be sold year after year

6. Publishing an academic book can lead to writing trade books, magazine articles and other works.

7. The possibility exists to expand into other lucrative and fulfilling ventures.

Disadvantages

1. In some subject areas, there are only a few major publishers.

2. In traditional subject areas, publishers may have a full stable.

3. A high level of organizational ability is required.

4. Technical accuracy and exactness is vital.

5. A great deal of time is required.

6. A substantial monetary investment may be necessary in research and materials.

7. Often, no advance is paid or the advance is low.

8. From the time the manuscript is started, it may take two to three years before any royalty income is received.

9. The possibility exists that the book may not sell well and that royalty income will be low.

Income Potential

If the book sells well, the income can be steady and high. A reasonable range might be $5,000 to $50,000 per year. Royalty rates vary, but 10 to 15% of the publisher's net receipts (about 80% of the list price) is a normal range for hardcover books, and 6 to 10% of the publisher's net receipts is normal for text-workbooks and other disposable materials.

BOOKS – FICTION

The term 'fiction' includes western, mystery, fantasy, science fiction, suspense and other types of stories. A novel usually runs from 50,000 to 120,000 words.

Advantages

1. There are an unlimited number of plots and stories.
2. Often no technical background, training or experience is required.
3. Often less research is required than when writing non-fiction.
4. A large number of publishing companies publish fiction.
5. There is a big reader demand for fiction.
6. The possibility exists for the sale of both hardcover and paperback rights.

7.   The possibility exists for book club sales, magazine reprint rights and movie rights.

Disadvantages

1.   Publishers receive many thousands of proposals and manuscripts annually.
2.   Usually a great deal of time and effort is required to complete a salable book.
3.   A high degree of creativity is required to complete a salable book.
4.   Strong organizational ability is required.
5.   A great deal of research may be required to accurately describe settings, events and conditions.
6.   From the time a manuscript is accepted for publication, it may be one to one and a half years before the book reaches the shelves.
7.   From the time a book reaches the shelves, it may be another year or more before any royalties are distributed.
8.   If the book does not sell well, you may not receive any royalty income beyond the advance.

Income Potential

Income potential can be very good. A previously unpublished author might expect an advance in the $1,000 to $10,000 range. Royal rates vary, but 10 to 15% of the cover price is a normal range for paperbacks.

BOOKS – ROMANCE NOVELS

A romance novel is a love story with a plot involving emotional conflict and resolution. The length typically runs from 50,000 to 100,000 words. 65,000 words is a good length.

Advantages

1.   There is a tremendous reader demand for new romance novels.
2.   Reader demand for romance novels continues to grow, despite the sagging overall book market.
3.   Publishers produce a large number of romance novels every year.
4.   Many different publishing companies produce romance novels. Several major publishers have added romance lines and this trend will probably continue.

5. No particular technical or educational background is required to write a romance novel.
6. Publishers are actively seeking good, new romance novel writers.
7. Many romance novels are relatively short. They take less time to write than many other types of full-length fiction.
8. Once a writer figures out the 'formula,' they can produce many books in a relatively short time.
9. There is the possibility of books club sales, magazine reprints and movie rights sales.
10. Romance is an enduring topic. Love is here to stay.

Disadvantages

1. There are a large number of romance manuscripts being produced by would-be authors. It can be difficult to break in.
2. There is a definite knack to writing a romance novel. You must understand how to format a romance novel.
3. Story lines, plots, settings and types of characters are somewhat trendy. You must determine what is 'in' and what is not.
4. The market is flooded with romance novels. Even if a romance novel gets published, it may not sell well.
5. There may be a time lag of one to one and a half years from when the manuscript is completed to when royalty income is received.

Income Potential

Income potential can be excellent. Advances for previously unpublished authors range from about $2,500 to $10,000. Royalty rates range from 6% to 8% of the cover price. A first printing may consist of 50,000 to 100,000 copies.

BOOKS – FOR CHILDREN

Children's books can cover a wide range, from heavily-illustrated 'picture books' (age 2-6) to juveniles (ages 8-12) to books for youth (ages 12-15). Topics vary widely. The same writing principles that apply to books for adults also apply to children's books.

Advantages

1. Many publishers produce books for children, juveniles and youth.

2. No particular educational background or technical expertise is required to write children's fiction books.
3. Books for young children are usually short (24, 32, 48 or 64 pages) and there is very little copy. A children's picture book may have 500 to 2,500 words. A juvenile book might have 15,000 to 40,000 words. Youth books might range from 15,000 to 75,000. Since these books are often shorter than other types of books, the writer's time investment will most likely be less.
4. There is a wide range of topics and types of books to consider for a manuscript.
5. Well-written children's books can endure, with continued sales for many years.

Disadvantages

1. Although many children's, juvenile and youth books are published, the huge mass market that other types of books enjoy is not readily available.
2. Since no particular background or training is necessary, there are many would-be authors eager to break in, including teachers. Competition is stiff.
3. The writer must be in tune with children's interests.
4. Plots and events must be within the readers' level of comprehension.
5. The author must know and conform to the correct reading level, and must be careful in word selection.
6. The writer must be aware of specific techniques that should be used in writing books for readers of this age.

Income Potential

Income can be good, but often not as high as with other types of books. Even if an advance is paid, it will be considerably less than for other types of books. The royalty rate may range from 5 to 10% of the cover price. If an illustrator is involved, the royalty may be split between the author and the illustrator.

NEWSPAPERS – ARTICLES

Good possibilities exist to write for a local or regional newspaper on a freelance basis or as a special-feature writer. News items, human-interest stories and people-profiles are good freelance possibilities. Regular features on gardening, investments, local entertainment, newcomers to the community or similar topics have great potential.

Advantages

1. It's possible to make personal contact with newspaper publishers.
2. It's an excellent way to sharpen your writing skills.
3. You see almost immediate results.
4. You get paid for the photographs you take.
5. It's a good way to establish writing credits and build your portfolio.
6. A steady income can develop, though it probably won't be high.
7. You will gain a local or regional reputation as a writer. Other possibilities will exist to expand into more lucrative freelance writing in your area.

Disadvantages

1. You are still a long way from having a major publication on a national level.
2. Income is usually lower than that which is possible from writing other types of material.

Income Potential

Income can be low, perhaps $15 to $30 for a local article and $50 + for an article in a regional publication.

POETRY

Poetry is usually written for the sheer pleasure of it.

Advantages

1. Poetry, more often than not, is written for the pleasure it brings to the writer and his/her readers.
2. Writing poetry is a good way to sharpen writing skills.
3. It's a good way to develop skills as a lyricist (songwriter).
4. Personal satisfaction and a feeling of accomplishment are achieved by seeing your work in print.
5. The possibility exists to enter and win poetry contests.

Disadvantages

1. There is a limited commercial market for poetry. Many publishers do not publish books of poetry. Many major magazines do not publish

2.   poetry. The best market is with 'little magazines,' (magazines with a low circulation – say 5,000 or less).

Income Potential

Some publications that use poetry pay nothing. Most others pay very little.

SCRIPTS – TELEVISION AND MOVIES

Television and movie scripts include the entire plot, settings and dialogue for television programs and movies.

Advantages

1.   There are many agents who handle scripts and who can be contacted.
2.   There is a high prestige factor.
3.   Income from a unique, high-quality, first-rate script can be outstanding.
4.   The possibility exists to produce a book or magazine articles based on the script. Usually, however, the script is based on a book rather than the book (novelization) being based on the movie.

Disadvantages

1.   Since a producer may invest millions of dollars producing a movie or television program, your work must be of a high enough quality and unique enough in nature to inspire multi-million dollar faith and confidence.
2.   Most scripts are sold through agents. Thus, you must first sell an agent on your project and then the agent must sell a producer on it.
3.   Most of the top agents will not even look at unsolicited manuscripts.
4.   This is a specialized area and you must thoroughly know your craft.
5.   A substantial time investment is required.

Income Potential

Television scripts are usually purchased outright. The pay range for a 60-minute telescript is usually $20,000 to $30,000. Feature length movie scripts are either purchased for 'development' or purchased outright. A scriptwriter might be paid $5,000 to $50,000 for a script that goes into development. It's possible that similar substantial amounts may be collected as it remains in

development. Scripts that are purchased outright can range from $50,000 to $2,000,000. Often, scripts are purchased outright in the $500,000 to $1,000,000 range. Scriptwriters who are hired to work on scripts in development or to rewrite scripts in production (script doctors) might be paid a fee of $50,000 to $1,000,000 per script.

> "Easy reading is damn hard writing."
> Nathaniel Hawthorne

SONGS – LYRICS

A lyricist writes words for songs. Ideally, the lyricist should also write melodies or should collaborate with a melody writer to produce finished songs for submission.

Advantages

1. There are many artists, producers, song publishers and recording companies looking for 'hit' songs.
2. There is usually a relatively small time investment. Some hit songs have been written in a 5-minute flash of inspiration. 'Grinding out'
3. the lyrics to a song may take only a few hours for an experienced lyricist.
4. It's a good commercial market for poets to consider.
5. Fame and fortune are possible.
6. It's a good way to ease into a career as a performer, independent record producer or other music-related activities.

Disadvantages

1. There are many would-be songwriters. Competition is stiff.
2. Ideally, a fully orchestrated demo is prepared for submission of a song. This can be costly.
3. Music producers and performers are looking for 'hit quality' material. Whereas it may be easy to write a song, a *great* song is difficult to write.
4. Income can be sporadic, and low, if salable songs are not produced regularly.

Income Potential

Income is earned from record sales, music publishing and performance rights.

a. Publishing rights are assigned to a publisher and the writer in turn receives payment through the publisher. The songwriter receives 3 to 5% of the cover price of sheet music sold and 10% on choral arrangements and orchestrations sold. This money comes through the publisher.

b. Performance rights organizations (BMI, ASCAP, SESAC) collect performance payments from radio and television stations, night clubs and others who utilize music for profit. In turn, these organizations make payment to writers of 'logged' songs, who are a member of their organization.

BUSINESS AND INDUSTRY

Good possibilities exist to write newsletters, brochures, sales manuals, booklets, sales letters, advertising copy and the like for businesses in your area.

Advantages

1. It's a good way to sharpen organizational ability and writing skills.
2. There is usually a short time lag from when the work is completed to when payment is received.

Disadvantages

1. You will probably receive little or no credit for your efforts.
2. It's a good way to earn money, but you are still not a bona fide 'author.'

Income Potential

Income can be good and steady. Rates might range from $25 to $50 or more per hour.

FILLERS

Fillers are short pieces, such as anecdotes, humor, household hints, bumper stickers, road signs, recipes, humorous happenings, jokes, children's comments and other odds and ends that newspaper and magazine publishers use to 'fill up' columns.

<u>Advantages</u>

1. Many newspapers and magazines buy these.
2. There's a small time investment per filler.
3. It's a good way to get into print.
4. It's a good way to earn some money, though payment is usually small.
5. It's a good way to sharpen your writing skills.
6. Simultaneous submissions are usually acceptable.

<u>Disadvantages</u>

1. Your submission will most likely appear with no byline.
2. You will most likely receive no comment from a publisher unless they use your material. Unused material is not sent back. Follow-up would probably be pointless.

<u>Income Potential</u>

Payment for a short piece may only be a few dollars.

FINDING YOUR "NICHE"

> "My parents had an inkling of what I might become when I was five years old. When they read me 'Humpty Dumpty,' I asked, 'Was he pushed?'"
> Mystery writer P.D. James

Ask yourself the following questions. Your answers will help you identify the ideal writing medium to pursue.

1. What type of educational background, technical knowledge and expertise do you possess?
2. What do you like to read?
3. What do you like to write?
4. How much time can/will you devote to a project?
5. What type of writing fits your personality?
6. What types of writing skills do you possess or are willing to develop?
7. What types of publishing mediums are best suited for the type of work you plan to create?
8. What are your goals as a writer?
   a. A hobby or a business?
   b. To see your name in print, or to get published and make money?
   c. What are your writing income goals?
   d. Are your writing career plans short-term or long-term?

MANUSCRIPT DEVELOPMENT

GENERAL GUIDELINES

The following comments pertain to any type of manuscript.

Elements of the Manuscript

Regardless of the type of writing that you do, know these elements of your manuscript.

Topic
The topic is the subject of your manuscript, more narrowly defined.
1. Develop a clear vision of your topic.
   a. What are you trying to communicate?
   b. Where are your ideas going?
2. Develop a broad or detailed outline of your plot or of topics and subtopics to be included.
   a. Organize the outline in logical order.
3. Develop a slant or approach for your manuscript.

A *subject* of a research paper is the general content. Subjects are broad and general. For example:

- Health
- Television
- Stocks and bonds
- Travel

The *topic* of a research paper, in contrast, is the specific issue being discussed. Here are some possible topics for a research paper developed from the previous subjects:

- **Health**
  Assessing fad diets

  Arguing the merits of AIDS testing of healthy care workers

- **Television**
  Arguing for or against the V-chip in television

  Taking a side in the cable wars

- **Stocks and Bonds**
  Showing that day trading is profitable (or not)

  Persuading readers to use e-trades rather than brokers (or vice versa)

- **Travel**
  Arguing that surcharges for solo travelers is unfair

  Arguing the merits of e-tickets

Market Research

Market research is conducted to determine if there is a reader audience for your manuscript, and to determine if it a publisher will be interested in publishing your work.

1. Determine the market potential.
   a. Is there a market for this manuscript?
   b. Is the market already flooded?
   c. Can I develop a new slant or approach to this topic that will fit into a 'niche' that is not currently being reached?
   d. How many potential publishers are there for me to contact?
   e. Will this idea have broad or limited appeal?
   f. Check these sources:
      1. Amazon.com; search by category.
      2. *Reader's Guide to Periodical Literature, Subject Guide to Books in Print,* and other appropriate indexes. Can be found in most libraries.
      3. Writer's market guides, such as *Writer's Market, Literary Marketplace* (LMP) and *Children's Writer's and Illustrator's Market.*

Format

Format is the arrangement of the parts of the manuscript.

1. For nonfiction, devise a system of units, chapters and other appropriate dividers.
2. Devise a system of headings and subheadings.
3. Develop an order for your manuscript. Present like materials in the same way under the same heading levels.
4. Be consistent with your format throughout the manuscript.
5. Consider how you will use examples, sidebars, illustrations and the like.

Content

Content is what is included in your manuscript. Decide how thoroughly you will explain each topic.

1. The makeup of your reader audience and the nature of your topic will provide a good guide.
2. Be as concise as possible. Do not tell everything you know. Provide only that which is absolutely necessary for the reader to be told.
3. Do not leave out essential information that must be revealed to the reader in order for them to reach the proper conclusion.

Style

Style is your voice, how you express your ideas.

1. Develop your own personal style/voice.
2. Use a writing style that is within generally acceptable limits.
3. Write in a style that is normal for the type of work you are preparing.
4. If you are preparing a manuscript for submission to a particular publication, gear your writing toward the writing style found in that publication.

Outlining

Not every successful author works from an outline. Some prefer to start with an idea and let it take them where it may. But a clear outline can help an author organize, both for fiction and nonfiction. If you choose to outline, remember that most novels are written using the Three-Act Structure.

Act 1

1. Hook: A gripping plot event that pulls the reader in and gets him involved in the story.
2. Backstory: A bridge that introduces the protagonist, fills the reader in and lays the groundwork for plot and story.
3. Trigger: An event that propels the protagonist into crisis.

Act 2

1. Crisis: The protagonist suffers an emotional crisis because of the trigger's effect on a character flaw.
2. Struggle: The protagonist struggles against ever-increasing obstacles.
3. Epiphany: The protagonist realizes his/her flaw and overcomes it (or not).

Act 3

1. Plan: The protagonist does something he/she couldn't do before the epiphany.
2. Climax: The protagonist confronts the antagonist, who (or which) is defeated.
3. Ending: The plot and story conflicts are resolved, and the reader is left satisfied.

STORY & PLOT

Without a story, your novel is nothing more than a series of meaningless plot events. And without plot, your character's emotions would exist in a meaningless context. Every novel, screenplay or other work of fiction needs both story and plot to be successful.

STORY is emotional. When your character feels sad, that's part of the story. Some elements of story are:

Anger * Joy * Fear * Desire * Sorrow

PLOT is physical. When your character cries, that's part of the plot. Some elements of plot are:

Plan * Speed * Danger * Thrills * Conflict

It's important to balance plot and story. You need both, and one leads to the other. A rough example:

Plot:
After accidentally shooting an innocent bystander, (Hook)
Story:
a police detective is tormented with guilt.
Plot:
He retires from the police force (Trigger)
Story:
too ashamed to face his coworkers.
Plot:
He descends into alcoholism and struggles to pay the bills, (Crisis)
Story:
aware that he's on a downward slide but helpless to stop it. (Struggle)
Plot:
When he is hired to do some investigating on the side, he encounters a drug addict who is stealing to support his habit.
Story:
Seeing himself reflected in the addict's miserable life, the detective vows to quit drinking. He confronts the events that caused his guilt, retrieving long-forgotten memories of the accidental shooting. (Epiphany)

Plot:

But now the addict is after him.

Story:

Feeling stronger through self-discover, the detective confronts the addict, (Plan)

Plot:

fights with him and holds him until the police arrive. (Climax)

Story:

Sober and with newfound confidence (Ending)

Plot:

he starts his own private detective agency.

End

Titles

Follow these guidelines in selecting a title for your manuscript.

1. Whether short or long, make it catchy and attention-getting.
2. Use a subtitle, in nonfiction, to more fully explain the title and the manuscript.
3. Make the title relevant. The title should reflect the content of the article or book.
4. Don't be so clever that the average reader cannot understand the title or can't draw the association between title and manuscript content.

Production Rate

Production rate refers to the volume of material produced in a given time.

1. There is no standard production rate. Some successful authors regularly spend days on a single paragraph. Others routinely crank out a romance novel every couple of months.
2. To produce an adequate volume of material, follow these suggestions:
   a. Write regularly. Set aside a time to write each day or each week, and stick to your schedule.
   b. Set a goal of a certain number of pages per day or per week.

Collaborating

There are both advantages and disadvantages to working with a co-author. Some factors to consider are listed here.

Advantages

1. More and better ideas.
2. Complementary skills result in an easier task.
3. Division of workload.
4. More viewpoints and better perspective.
5. More enthusiasm; more fun.

Disadvantages

1. Possible complications with the following:
   a. Conflicting philosophies about the project's direction.
   b. Conflicting work habits.
   c. Amount of work produced by each partner.
   d. Incompatibility and infighting.
2. Maintaining consistent style, tone and approach.
3. Logistics.
4. Split credits.
5. Divided income.

Finding a Co-Author

1. Consider your co-workers.
2. Contacts made at seminars and workshops.
3. Contact published authors of newspaper articles, books or magazine articles.
4. Browse online sites where writers advertise their availability, such as:

   www.Online-writing-jobs.com

   www.guru.com

   www.elance.com

Situations Where Co-Authoring Might be Ideal

1. Where you need one of the following:
   a. Illustrator / artist
   b. Photographer
   c. Expert in the field
   d. Ghostwriter

Use of a Pseudonym

A pseudonym is a pen name under which an author's works are published.

Why Use a Pseudonym?

1. To protect a writer's identity from friends, business associates, etc.
2. If your real name is 'plain.'
3. For different types of works.

Selecting a Pen Name

1. Do not select a pen name used by another published author.
   a. Check the Library of Congress Catalog Directory of Authors at a library.
   b. Enter a name in Amazon.com and see what comes up.
2. Do not select the name of a famous person.
3. If you select a real person's name, change the spelling or use a selection or combination of names.

> "It is impossible to discourage the real writers. They don't give a damn what you say, they're going to write."
> Sinclair Lewis

SPECIFIC GUIDELINES

Following are some guidelines and tips for specific types of writing.

Fiction

1. Develop the framework of your plot before you begin writing.
2. Develop a synopsis of the entire short story or book. Then, also develop a summary of each section or chapter.

3. Create reader identification. That is, develop a plot, characters and feelings with which the reader can identify. Your readers should be able to project themselves into the story.
4. Keep the story believable.
5. There must be a significant challenge, conflict or struggle involved in your plot as the characters pursue their goals and dreams to achieve wealth, victory, happiness or love.
6. Develop strong, believable characters.
7. Develop likable characters that, though flawed, your readers can admire and root for.
8. Know your characters. Know their backgrounds, likes, dislikes, how they react, their motivations, their activities – everything about them.

 1. You will find it helpful to write a detailed sketch of each character.
 2. When writing the manuscript, constantly ask yourself:
  1. How would they respond to this situation?
  2. What are they *really* after?

9. Keep the disposition, attitudes and nature of each character consistent throughout the manuscript. Likewise, be consistent in how your characters interact with each other.
10. Make the dialogue fit each character's age, position, role and self-concept.
11. Be certain your manuscript is technically accurate in factual material, descriptions of geographic locations, historical data, etc.

Children's Books

1. Develop a strong plot and believable characters, just as when writing other fiction.
2. Be aware of the interests, problems and attitudes of the children in the age group you are writing for.
3. Make your vocabulary selection and sentence structures appropriate for the target audience's reading level.
4. Follow the same guidelines as when developing any other type of similar fiction or nonfiction works.

Newspapers

1. Be objective. Your story should be a complete, accurate, undistorted report of the event you are writing about.
2. Be impartial. Present all points of view with the same degree of prominence.
3. Do not become strongly affiliated with groups or organizations that might cause you a conflict of interest or which might allow others to question your impartiality.
4. If there are conflicting points of view, or potentially damaging allegations, give each party involved a chance to present their side of the story.

> "What people are ashamed of usually makes a good story."
> F. Scott Fitzgerald

MANUSCRIPT MECHANICS

MANUSCRIPTS FOR BOOKS AND MAGAZINES

Use this format for preparing manuscripts for books, magazine articles, shorts stories and novels.

Paper

1. White, 8 ½" x 11", 20 pound weight.

2. No erasable bond.

Word Processor or Typewriter

1. Use a good, letter-quality inkjet or laser printer. Do not use a dot matrix printer.

2. If using a typewriter, use a good, fresh ribbon.

3. If using a typewriter, pica is preferred over elite.

4. If using a typewriter, erasing, strike-over paper or liquid paper is acceptable. If there are several error corrections per page, retype. If using a computer and printer, reprint.

5. Use a standard type style. Times New Roman is preferred; Arial is acceptable. Do not use script, italics or unusual styles. The exception is italics for the emphasis of individual words.

Format

1. Type on one side of the paper only.

2. Double-space the entire manuscript.

3. A title page can be used for a book manuscript. Include the manuscript title, your name and address, the approximate word count.

4. On page two and subsequent pages, leave about one inch as a top margin above the page number. After the page number, triple space before resuming the manuscript.

5. Set side margins at 1 ¼ to 1 ½" wide.

6. Set bottom margin at 1 ¼ to 1 ½" inches.

Poetry

1. Type each poem on a separate sheet of paper.

2. Use white, 8 ½" x 11" bond paper, 20 pound weight.

3. Type your name and address in the upper left-hand corner.

4. Center the heading above the poem.

5. If it's a short poem, double-space. If it's a long poem, single-spacing is preferred to using two pages.

6. Center the poem vertically and horizontally on the page.

7. Type your name below the poem so it ends near your right margin.

8. Usually 10 to 15 poems can be submitted at a time.

Fillers

1. Type each item on a separate sheet of paper.

2. Use white, 8 ½" x 11" bond paper, 20 pound weight.

3. Use standard manuscript format.

4. Type your name, address and phone number in the upper left-hand corner. Type the approximate word count in the upper right-hand corner.

Mary Jones
125 Orchard Lane
Midwest, IA 51xxx
712-xxx-xxxx
MJJones@sample.com

Romance
60,000 words

LOVE'S MANY FACES

By Lolita Sinclair

Mary Jones
125 Orchard Lane
Midwest, IA 51xxx
712-xxx-xxxx
MJJones@sample.com

Approx. 4,200 words

LOVE'S MANY FACES

By Lolita Sinclair

Use this format for the first page of your magazine article, short story,

newspaper article or children's picture book. The title is placed one-third of the

way down the page. If a pseudonym is used, it appears in the byline and the writer's

real name is shown in the return address area in the upper left-hand corner. Show

the approximate number of words of the manuscript at the upper right-hand corner.

Don't justify the right margins, and always double-space.

Several different styles are acceptable for the second page heading of your manuscript. Here's one. Whatever format you use, make sure you use it consistently on every page of your manuscript.

Leave a one-inch top margin above the heading on page two and subsequent pages. After the heading, triple space, leaving two blank lines before continuing with the text of the manuscript.

SUBMITTING YOUR WORK

QUERY LETTERS

A query letter is sent to a publisher or literary agent. It serves to briefly describe your manuscript idea and asks if you may submit more material for an editor's review. Note: some publishers / agents prefer that you submit the first three chapters of your work, or even the entire work with your letter. Check market guides for editorial preferences.

Finding the Right Publisher

1. Know your manuscript.
   a. What is its topic and slant?
   b. To what type of reader will it appeal?
   c. For what publishing medium is it best suited?

2. Familiarize yourself with publishers that publish your type of work.
   a. Browse through bookstores and libraries.
   b. Browse Amazon.com and BarnesandNoble.com.
   c. Check the *Subject Guide to Books in Print*.
   d. Check your local library.
   e. Check market guidebooks like *Writer's Market* and *Literary Marketplace.*

3. From a market guide, determine publisher's attitudes toward queries and their requirements for submitting them. Adhere to their requests.
4. Make a list of potential publishers, complete with addresses and editors' names. Rank them in category, from most ideal to least ideal.
5. Query the most ideal publishers first.
6. Consider making multiple queries.

Query Letter Philosophies and Procedures

The information below provides perspectives and philosophies about query letters and describes how to use them.

Purpose of the Query Letter

1. Present your idea and sell the editor on its being a good idea.
2. Demonstrate your writing ability.
3. Obtain permission to submit more material.
4. Begin a dialogue with an editor.

Manuscript Development Before Query

1. With a non-fiction book, you can send a query letter and proposal after developing your basic idea and slant.
2. With fiction, for a beginning writer, you are expected to complete the entire manuscript before querying.
3. With a short story, you should have the manuscript completed.
4. With a short magazine article, you should have the manuscript completed.
5. With a long magazine article, you should, at a minimum, have your theme and slant developed.

Content of Query Letter

1. If you have impressive publishing credits, emphasize them.
2. Summarize the manuscript topic.
3. Explain your particular approach.
4. Evaluate the project's relevance.
5. Estimate the project's completed length.
6. Include whether or not the project is completed.
7. Summarize your background.
8. You may include one or more of the following:
   a. Synopsis / Outline
   b. Market Analysis
   c. Samples of previous publications

Structure of the Query Letter

1. Use white, 8 ½" x 11" bond paper, 20 pound weight. 24 pound acceptable. If you have personalized letterhead paper, you may use it.

2.   Limit your letter to one page.
3.   Address the letter to a specific editor by name, if possible.
4.   Each letter should be original.
5.   Demonstrate your writing style and skill.
6.   Make certain there are no errors or obvious typographical corrections.
7.   Close with a request of some type of action from the editor.
8.   Enclose SASE.
9.   Be appreciative.

Realistic Expectations

1.   You will likely hear from most of the publishers queried. However, you might never hear from some of them.
2.   Most responses will be form letters.
3.   If your proposal is rejected, it's likely you will not be given a specific reason.
4.   If you have selected a good topic and have developed an enticing query letter and proposal, one or more publishers may ask to see your work.
5.   If you submit your completed manuscript (or sample), upon an editor's request, you are making progress, but you are still a long way from having a contract.
6.   Hang in there!

"If my doctor told me I had only six months to live, I wouldn't brood. I'd type a little faster."
  Isaac Asimov

Follow-Up

1.   Normal response time:
       a.   Magazines: 6 to 12 weeks.
       b.   Books: 3 to 9 months.
2.   Follow-up procedure:
       a.   Send a follow-up letter after a reasonable time.

Record

1.   Maintain records of names and addresses of publishers and the date on which the query letter was sent.
2.   Record the publisher response.
3.   Record follow-up information.

(SAMPLE QUERY LETTER)

Date

Editor's Name, Editorial Assistant (or title)
Name of Company
Street
City, State, Zip

Dear xxxxx:

After Stella Sebastian accidentally runs over the handsome photographer she's recently met, breaking his leg, she must spend the rest of her vacation driving him around to various photo shoots. Recently divorced, Stella is not looking to get involved, and she remains distrustful of relationships in general. Reid Beckman's experience as a photographer for the AP in Iraq has left him scarred, and doubting his ability to see the beauty in the world around him. He wants only to lay low and try to put the experience behind him. But when he meets Stella, Reid is drawn to the lovely, spirited woman despite his efforts to remain detached. As they get to know each other, Stella and Reid must each let go of past wounds in order for love to flourish.

AS EAGLES SOAR is my recently completed 57,000-word romance novel. As a longtime fan of romances, I believe AS EAGLES SOAR would be suitable for the Harlequin American Romance line.

I've published seven novels, all under the name Jean Simon. These were released between 1987 and 1994. The first was a YA romance with Silhouette; the rest were occult/suspense published by Random House and Kensington.

Enclosed please find a short synopsis and first three chapters of AS EAGLES SOAR. SASE is included for your reply. Thank you for your time, and I look forward to hearing from you.

Sincerely,

Your Name
Address
City, State
Phone
Email

AGENTS

At some point in your writing career, you will probably consider the use of an agent to place your work.

Agent's Activities

1. An agent's job is to place the author's manuscript with the most suitable publisher. Sometimes agents also help promote and publicize the author's work.
2. Agents will handle both established authors with publishing credits to their name, and unpublished writers.
3. Agents usually handle only books, and television and movie scripts. There is not enough money involved in magazine articles, short stories, poetry and the like to make it worth their while.
4. Agents charge 10% to 15% of the author's gross earnings for placing works with a domestic publisher and, usually, another 5% for placing works with a foreign publisher.
5. Some agents charge a reading fee for reviewing a prospective client's manuscript. Respectable agents do not charge reading fees.

How to Find an Agent

1. The following publications contain lists of book and screenplay agents:

   Writer's Market, published by Writer's Digest Books

   Literary Marketplace, published by Information Today

   Guide to Literary Agents published by Writer's Digest Books
   Jeff Herman's Guide to Book Publishers, Editors & Literary Agents by Jeff Herman

Why to Use an Agent

1. Publishers are more willing to look at work submitted by an agent, because they know the work has merit.

2.   Your agent will make sure you receive your full royalties due in a timely manner.

3.   Your agent will help resolve any creative differences that might arise between you and the publisher.

Why Not to Use an Agent

1.   It may be just as difficult and time-consuming to land an agent who will handle your work as it would be to place the work yourself.

2.   If you place your work without the aid of an agent, you'll save 10 – 15% of the royalties paid.

3.   Even if you land an agent, they may not give you and your work a satisfactory amount of attention.

4.   You can gain valuable experience and insight by handling your own marketing.

"Writing is utter solitude, the descent into the cold abyss of oneself."
  Franz Kafka

THE AUTHOR'S CONTRACT

Someday you may be fortunate enough to – finally! – sign a publishing contract. When that day comes, there are a few things you should know.

What the Publisher Agrees to do for You

1. Publish your book within a fixed time frame, usually 12 to 18 months from the time you deliver the signed contract.

2. Allow you to review and correct galley proofs of your work.

3. Consult with you regarding book jacket, blurbs and your author biography and photo.

4. Pay your advances in a prompt manner, and royalties twice a year.

What the Publisher Does NOT Agree to Do

1. Market your book.

2. Give you final say over the book jacket design.

3. Guarantee a certain print run.

What You Agree to Do

1. Deliver a book of an agreed length, genre and subject matter, before the agreed-upon date.

2. Confirm that the book is your original work, and that you aren't libeling anyone with it.

> "We are what we repeatedly do. Excellence, therefore, is not an act but a habit."   Aristotle

PROTECTING YOUR WORK

Securing a Copyright

Idea and concepts cannot be copyrighted, but your expression of those ideas can be. That is, the specific combination of words you use to express your ideas and concepts are protected by copyright. Illustrations, photographs and other artwork are also protected by copyright.

Material published after March 1, 1989 is automatically copyrighted when written and doesn't need a copyright notation.

Even though a copyright notation is not needed, many writers affix the notation anyway, as shown below, when showing their work to the general public, to fend off those who might be tempted to copy their work.

Copyright © 2008, Jean Tennant

Do NOT include the copyright notation when submitting your work to a literary agent or publisher. It's considered the sign of an amateur.

To establish your proof of ownership, register your copyright online at:

www.copyright.gov

or through the following address:

U.S. Copyright Office
Library of Congress
101 Independence Avenue, SE
Washington, DC 20559-6000

Copyright forms are free, available online through the above sources, or you can call 202-707-9100 to request a form. To speak to someone at the copyright office about specific copyright questions,

call 202-707-3000. The correct forms to use to register various types of works are:

Form TX: Written works, including book manuscripts, magazine articles, short stories and poetry.

Form PA: Plays and music

Form VA: Illustrations and photographs

Send one copy of your work, the completed copyright registration form and a $45 fee to the U.S. Copyright Office. The copyright office will date your copyright applications soon after it is received. You'll receive a copy of the copyright registration, bearing your registration number. It may take as long as six months to receive your copy of the form.

The Berne Convention, ratified by the U.S. Congress in 1989, gives copyright protection in the U.S. and eighty other countries.

A copyright lasts for the author's lifetime plus 70 years. If you have a co-author or collaboration with an illustrator, the copyright lasts the lifetime of the last survivor plus 70 years. If you use a pseudonym, the copyright protection lasts for 100 years or for 75 years after publication, whichever is shorter.

Selling Rights

Various types of serial rights can be sold to works published in magazines and newspapers. The term serial means those publications that are published on a continual basis, like magazines and newspapers. Some of the more common serial rights are listed below:

The term First Serial Rights means that the first rights to publish in the U.S. only are being granted.

The term First North American Serial Rights means that first rights are granted for publication in North America (U.S. and Canada).

The terms <u>Second Serial Rights</u> and <u>Second North American Serial Rights</u> refer to the right to publish a book excerpt in a magazine

after the book is published. The terms also are used to identify subsequent sales to magazines or newspapers of a published article or story where first rights were granted to the original publisher. Second rights can be sold any number of times by the copyright holder.

The term <u>All Rights</u> refers to the sale of all rights to the author's work. Thereafter, the author is unable to sell second rights to other users.

The term <u>One-Time Rights</u> refers to the author's giving a publication permission to publish the material one time, and then all rights revert to the copyright holder. The publisher receives no guarantee that they are the only one, or the first one, to receive permission to publish the material.

The term <u>Simultaneous Rights</u> refers to granting the right to more than one publisher to publish your work, all at the same time or with no regard for who publishes the work first.

#1 MOST IMPORTANT THING TO REMEMBER: NEVER GIVE UP!

> "I would credit my success as an author not to any great talent, in particular, but through sheer stubborn determination."

NOTES

NOTES

33818607R00060

Made in the USA
Lexington, KY
11 July 2014